Traditions Around The World
Masks

by Amanda Earl and Danielle Sensier

an imprint of Hodder Children's Books

Traditions Around The World

Other titles in the Traditions Around The World series:

Body Decoration

Costumes

Dance

Food

Games

Jewellery and Accessories

Musical Instruments

Series editor: James Kerr

Designer: Loraine Hayes

Consultant: Anthony Shelton, Keeper of Non-Western Art and Anthropology, Royal Pavilion Art Gallery and Museums, Brighton, East Sussex, England.

First published in 1994 by Wayland (Publishers) Ltd
This paperback edition published in 2001 by Hodder Wayland, an imprint of Hodder Children's Books

© Hodder Wayland 1994

British Library Cataloguing in Publication Data

Sensier, Danielle
  Masks. - (Traditions Around the World Series)
  I. Title II. Earl, Amanda III. Series
  391.434

ISBN 0 7502 3440 7

Typeset by Loraine Hayes Design
Printed and bound in Italy by G. Canale and C.S.p.A.

COVER: A *tatanua* mask from the Pacific.

Picture acknowledgements:

The publishers wish to thank the following for providing the photographs for this book: Brighton Museum and Art Gallery 34; © British Museum 40, 45; Bruce Coleman Limited COVER, 14-15, 16, 17, 18 and 19 (Frans Lanting), 28-29 (Norman Myers) 40-41, 44-45; Robert Estall 39 (© Angela Fisher); Explorer 12, 37; Eye Ubiquitous 8 (© Eric Enstone), 28, 43; The Hutchison Library 10-11, 26-27, 27, 29, 35; Life File 11 (Jeremy Hoare), 14 (Sally-Ann Fison), 23 (Richard Powers), 24 (Jeremy Hoare); Link 15, 25 (Lourdes Grobet), 32; Tony Morrison 6-7, 21 (© Tony Morrison), 20-21, 22, 25; Edward Parker 6; Photri 30-31; Rock Graphics 38; Still Pictures 34-35, 36, 38-39; Tony Stone Worldwide 8-9; Tropix 42-43 (M. Jory).

Artwork by Peter Bull.

Contents

Masks around the world

NORTH AMERICA

SOUTH AMERICA

EUROPE

ASIA

AFRICA

THE PACIFIC

Introduction

Masks play an important part in many different traditions around the world. When people put on a mask they are usually disguising themselves, and can almost feel they have become another person, an animal, a ghost, or whatever the mask represents. In fact, in some religions it is believed that the wearer actually changes into a spirit or ancestor.

Masks are sometimes worn for fun at fancy dress parties, such as at Hallowe'en. At other times they are used in the theatre to help audiences identify different characters. In many parts of the world where carnivals and festivals are very popular, colourful masquerades are an important part of the celebrations.

For some people, masks are an essential part of their beliefs and customs. Elaborate masks are worn at religious ceremonies to mark an important event. This might be to celebrate a successful harvest, to appeal to spirits for rain, or at an initiation ceremony when a child is ready to become an adult.

An African mask. ▶

**Main picture:
In Central and South America, masks are worn at religious festivals and masquerades. At this market stall in Guatemala, a great variety of masks are for sale, representing ancestors, animal spirits and demons.**

▲ **A theatrical dance mask from Bali, Indonesia. This is Rangda, an evil character from the Barong dance dramas.**

People have used masks for many thousands of years. The oldest known mask, representing a coyote, was found in Mexico and is about 10,000 years old. Other masks found by archaeologists are from ancient Egyptian times, when masks were made for the mummified bodies of the dead.

Mask designs reflect the traditional art and crafts of the region in which they are made. They can have many different forms – animal, human or a mixture of both – and a variety of colours, textures and patterns.

Masks are usually made from the kind of natural materials that are easy to find locally. They vary from region to region, and range from bark cloth in Papua New Guinea to cowrie shells and feathers in Zaire. Today's mask-makers also use manufactured materials, such as light bulbs and rubber tubing.

Europe

Europe has many exciting masking traditions, usually linked to the changing of the seasons, religious celebrations or theatrical performances. In ancient Greek theatre, actors sometimes wore masks, and during the Renaissance, masks became fashionable at extravagant masked balls held by the European aristocracy. The famous masked carnival in Venice, Italy has been celebrated since medieval times. However, not all European masquerades have had such a long history. The Notting Hill Carnival in London was started in the 1960s by Afro-Caribbean people who had migrated to England.

Many masquerades in Britain mark the changes of the seasons. In parts of Oxfordshire, Gloucestershire and Scotland, mumming plays are performed around Christmas time. Mumming comes from the German

Main picture: At the Venice Carnival, the streets are filled with people wearing richly decorated masks. These are often worn as part of an extravagant costume.

In Cornwall, England, ▶ the beginning of the summer is celebrated at the Padstow Hobby Horse masquerade. This fearsome monster dances through the streets shouting 'Summer is a-cum today'.

word for mask, and mummers, or 'guisers' in Scotland, have to make sure nobody knows who they are. Each performer wears a hat which has long strips of newspaper coming down over the face, along with a costume also covered in strips. The portrayal of a victim being killed shows that winter has ended and spring has begun.

In the Welsh counties of Glamorgan and Dyfed, the end of summer is marked with the *Mari Lwyd* processions held in December and January. A masked figure, covered totally in canvas, carrying a carved horse's head on a pole, is a well-known visitor. The carved wooden mask has a snapping mouth and green glass eyes.

◀ An ugly witch mask from the *Schemenlaufen* Festival in Austria. Masks are worn to scare away winter and bring a good harvest.

At the Notting Hill Carnival in London, thousands ▶ of people perform dances, music and masquerades, known as *mas'*. Each *mas'* group has its own theme, which is changed every year. Stunning costumes and masks are skilfully crafted, following themes such as 'our arrival', 'colours of the rainbow' and 'birds of paradise'.

In Scotland, the history of the masked Burry Man of South Queensferry dates back to the 1740s. This strange figure is covered from head to foot in sticky green burrs from the burdock plant. Thousands of burrs are collected and fixed on to a loosely woven material, which is then modelled into a close-fitting mask and costume. The mask is crowned with a huge hat covered with seventy red roses. It is believed the tradition is linked to the safety of fishing fleets on their journeys.

In the *Silvesterkläuse* festival in Urnasch, Switzerland, masked 'spirits of the new year' go from house to house visiting people. It is thought the masked tradition was once a way of begging in disguise. It has now turned into a festival for people to show off their stunning masks and craft skills. There are three groups of masked figures: the *schöne* (the beautiful), the *wüeschte* (the ugly) and the *schö-wüeschte* (the less ugly). The masks represent men and women, but they are very heavy so are only worn by men.

Austria's most well-known masked festival is the *Schemenlaufen*. In medieval times, masked figures chased bad spirits away to make sure there was a good harvest. The festival is still held every three years in the town of Imst.

Strange and wonderful animal masks are popular in parts of eastern Europe. In Poland, the *Turon* mask is worn at harvest and fertility rituals held by farmers. The mask is named after a creature from Polish folk tales and is covered in animal skin, with goat or ram horns and shiny metal discs for eyes. It is a hobby-horse and is held on a pole, the person carrying it being disguised by a huge shroud of material. It has a large mouth, which is hinged, snapping open and shut when a cord is pulled. In Bulgaria, fox, bear and bird masks are worn at new year celebrations, which in the past were linked with the start of the new sowing and harvesting season. At the celebrations, masked animal figures have to jump high in the air as, in earlier years, it was believed the crops would grow as high as the highest jump.

◀ Many different styles of mask are worn at the Venetian Carnival. These are plague-doctor masks – the long noses were once thought to protect the wearer from disease.

Some of the most varied and beautifully crafted masks can be found at the Venetian Carnival in Italy. Along with processions of gondolas, and side-shows of every kind, thousands of Venetians and visitors alike join in this huge masquerade. The festivities go on for seven days, and date back to a lively, fun-filled medieval festival which took place just before the religious period of Lent, when people fasted for forty days. In fact, the words *carne vale* are the Latin words for 'farewell to meat'.

Venice becomes a big, open theatre, where people choose from a variety of masks and act as they please because their identity is hidden. There are *gnaghe* masks, which men wear to disguise themselves as women. Another of the favourite disguises is the *bautta* mask with its tricorn (three-sided) hat.

This mask is a black or white half-mask which is worn with a long cloak. In the past it was meant to be worn only by certain noblemen, but on one particular day it could be worn by both rich and poor alike. The plague-doctor mask, with its long, hooked nose, is worn with special clothes which were once thought to protect the wearer from the plague.

Masks are still used in Europe in some theatrical performances, including pantomimes. Pantomime masks are great fun, and are usually worn by the frightening characters, such as the giant Blundoor Boro in *Jack and the Beanstalk*. In today's performances of Shakespeare's plays such as *Much Ado About Nothing* and *A Midsummer Night's Dream*, masks are worn to disguise the characters, with comic results.

Project : Making a Venetian Carnival mask

You will need:
Large, old plastic bowl
Old newspapers (4 sheets)
Water
PVA glue
Cardboard box
Pencil
Scissors
Elastic
Paints
Paintbrushes

1 Tear up old newspaper into small pieces (about the size of a postage stamp), and place in a bowl. Soak the newspaper overnight with water.

2 Mash up the newspaper so it looks like wet bread. Pour and then squeeze out as much of the water as you can. Add some PVA glue and mix together, keeping the mixture fairly dry. This is now papier mâché.

3 On your cardboard, draw an oval shape the size of your face, and cut it out. Cut eyeholes, and pierce holes on either side of the mask with the scissors to thread the elastic through. Then build up the features on your mask with papier mâché: a fat nose, bulging cheeks and perhaps a wart or a boil! Cover the cardboard completely in papier mâché and allow it to dry in a warm place.

4 Paint your mask to make it look as if it were carved from wood, adding the grain of the wood, as well as colour to the lips and cheeks.

13

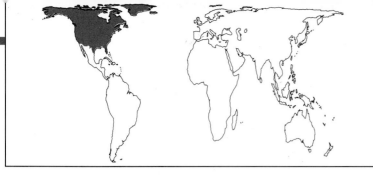

North America

In North America the most familiar masks are probably those worn at Hallowe'en – a popular time for mischief, fun and games. This festival dates back to the ancient Celts, who made human sacrifices to their gods at this time of year. Christians turned it into All Hallows' Eve, a frightening night when witches and devils were thought to walk the earth. It was introduced into the USA by British migrants in the eighteenth century, and today, all over the USA and Canada, people still disguise themselves as ghosts, witches and monsters. Children dress up for 'trick or treat', collecting sweets from neighbours in exchange for not playing tricks.

These children are wearing ▶ modern, mass-produced skeleton masks. They are celebrating Hallowe'en.

▲ Native American masks
are still worn today to help
keep old traditions alive.
These feather and cloth
masks are from New
Mexico, USA.

◄ This ghost monster mask
from Vancouver Island,
Canada, also looks like a
skeleton. Notice how hair has
been attached to the mask to
make it more realistic.

Long before the first migrants
arrived in North America, Native
Americans had their own masking
traditions. Unfortunately, few of these
have survived, as in the eighteenth and
nineteenth centuries many of these
people were killed or forced to abandon
their lands and traditions. However,
some now sell their masks to tourists,
helping to keep old skills alive as well as
to earn money. On the north-west
Pacific coast, groups such as the
Kwakiutl are performing their
masquerades once again.

A carved and painted ▶ eagle-spirit mask, made by the Haida people of the Pacific Northwest.

The Hopi are one of the Native American peoples of the Rio Grande. They now live mostly in villages on the Hopi Reservation in Arizona. They make money from cattle and sheep-rearing, tourism and arts and crafts, but they were traditionally crop farmers. This can be seen in their masquerades, which are linked to the sun and rain, a successful harvest and the change of the seasons throughout the year.

Hopi *Kachina* masks are worn at dance ceremonies, like the Bean and Water Serpent ceremonies in the spring, and the summer Home Dance ceremony. The masks represent mythical spirits that help the Hopi to summon rain. When a dancer wears a *Kachina* mask, he doesn't just look like the spirit, he believes that he actually becomes the spirit.

Today, the *Kachina* masks are usually helmet-shaped and are made of leather or hide, with an added framework of plywood for attaching ears, noses, snouts, horns and feather head-dresses. Some are decorated with painted symbols like budding corn, the sun, rain clouds and a rainbow. Others have human faces like the masks of hunters, girl warriors or grandmothers.

Along the north-west Pacific coast, from Washington State up to Yakutat Bay in Alaska, although traditional Native American lifestyles have almost disappeared, mask-making is still flourishing among local artists. Groups used to be divided into separate clans, each with their own masks given to them by mythical ancestors. These were a sign of the clan's authority – rather like European coats of arms. Many represented brave animal spirits, like the feathered eagle mask of the Nootka people. However, clans also honoured creatures such as the mouse, frog and woodworm. The masks were worn at *potlach* feasts, where the more noble the clan, the more numerous were the masks.

The thunderbird mask of the Kwakiutl people belongs to the *Hamatsa* clan. It represents a frightening forest spirit that assists the mythical cannibal monster, *Bakbakwal-anooksiwae*. As with many Kwakiutl masks, it has special moving parts which are operated by the dancer wearing it. The mask measures up to 2.4 m long, and has a huge beak which is snapped open and shut using pulleys and cords. It is carved from red cedar wood with fringes of cedar bark or animal skin.

After contact with outside traders, some Native American peoples began making masks to sell to European settlers. The Haida people were known for such masks, which were like portraits of real people. They even included carved moustaches, wrinkles and European beards and hairstyles.

On the other side of the continent, in the east, the carved wooden masks of the False Face Society are still worn among some of the Iroquois peoples. False Face masks are believed to prevent and cure illness, their power coming from the first False Face spirit, the Great Doctor. He is said to have broken his nose in a contest with the Creator of the World, and so False Face masks have a twisted look of pain. As a result of losing the contest, he was ordered to rid the earth of disease. So masks carved in his own image and hung with tiny bags of tobacco are said to have the power of healing – but only for illnesses of the head, such as nosebleeds and earache.

False Face ceremonies involve masked dancing, prayers and the burning of tobacco offerings. There are many rules about how False Face masks should be stored. If hung on a wall, a mask should always be covered or it may bring death. If it is not given regular offerings of tobacco, it is thought to bring bad luck, and if sold, it may come back to haunt its former owner. Some Iroquois believe that a fire in the New York State Museum in 1911 was caused by the museum not providing regular tobacco to the masks in its care.

◄ **This Kwakiutl eagle mask is another mythical spirit figure. It is made of carved wood, and has bird feathers to make it more realistic.**

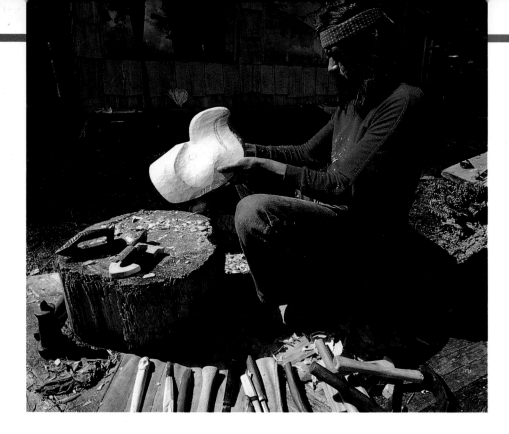

◄ Today's Native American artists still make wooden masks. This bird mask is being carved from a single piece of wood. It will be painted with traditional designs and will take many hours to complete.

In the harsh Arctic region, the Inuit people once performed masquerades during the long winter months. Although present-day Inuits are now mainly Christian, respect for the natural world is still very important, and traditional ideas still influence their way of life. Everything in the universe is believed to have its own spirit, called *inua*. Inuit masks represent these many different spirits, such as the sun and moon, giant animals or strange human beings. Several may be combined in one mask. Inuit masking traditions were also linked with hunting rituals. Each mask had its own special dance movements, performed to please the spirits of hunted animals.

Inuit masks are traditionally carved from driftwood, using beaver teeth and caribou antlers as tools. Many are surrounded by a band of wood, with holes at the edge for attaching anything that shakes and rattles, such as feathers, small wooden pendants, whalebone, or even strips of animal intestine. There were also female finger masks worn by women on their hands during dance ceremonies. They had round faces, eyes, teeth and hair, and were moved like puppets.

Traditional colours for masks were white, black, red and blue. Before contact with European traders, the Inuit used natural pigments made from sources like white clay, swamp grass and alder bark soaked in urine.

Today the Inuit do not follow masking traditions as they once did, although in the Nome area of Alaska, masks are still made to entertain tourists. In other parts of the region, local artists sell their carvings to city museums and art galleries, a trade that is becoming an important way for the Inuit to earn money.

Project: Making a Kwakiutl bird mask

You will need:
Large cardboard box
Pencil
Ruler
Scissors
Elastic
Compass
Masking tape
Ribbon
Paints
Coloured drinking straws
Feathers
30 cm dowel rod

1 Draw and then cut out the mask shape using the corner of the box, matching the width and length of your head.

2 Cut away the nose and mouth section, and cut out eyeholes. Pierce small holes at the sides and attach a piece of elastic to hold the mask on.

3 Draw and cut out the upper beak using another corner of the box. Do the same for the lower beak, making it smaller.

4 Using the compass, draw four circles: two at the bottom ends of the face mask and two at each side of the lower beak where it will join the mask. Cover all four circles with a few pieces of masking tape (to reinforce the cardboard), and pierce a hole through the centre of each circle.

5 Cut two strips of ribbon and thread each one through the matching holes. Tie a large knot at each end to stop the ribbon pulling through. This is the moving part of the beak.

6 Use the masking tape to attach the top beak to the mask. Paint the beak and the face of the mask in bands of bright colours. Stick straws behind the top of the mask and add feathers at intervals.

7 Attach the dowel rod to the bottom of the lower beak with masking tape, so that you can move the beak up and down.

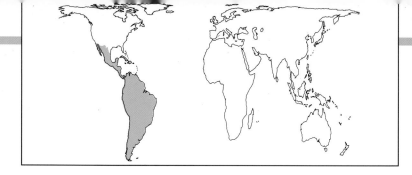

Central and South America

The masks of Central and South America have a very long history. Archaeologists believe they have existed since about 400 BC – 2,000 years before the Spanish conquests in the early sixteenth century. Many have been linked to the continent's ancient civilizations, such as the Aztecs of Mexico and the Incas of Peru. Rare Aztec masks of turquoise mosaic were found after the conquests, as well as decorated pottery showing masked figures at burial ceremonies.

Today, masking traditions are still widespread. Many are influenced by the beliefs of Amerindian peoples, who are the direct descendants of these ancient civilizations. Despite the near destruction of their race during the harsh colonial period, Amerindian peoples have survived and many are still living in the Andes and Mexico, as well as in remote areas of the Amazon Basin. They have strong beliefs in the power of nature and masking traditions are an important part of these beliefs. Animals, plants and the elements (such as rain and wind) are all thought to contain powerful spirits and ancestors. Masks are worn to represent them at many different ceremonies where people ask for help or try to please them with songs, dances and gifts.

One of Bolivia's many elaborate devil masks. ▶

The masks of the Tucuna people in northern Brazil are worn in female initiation rituals. These take place when Tucuna girls are ready to become adults. The wearing of Amerindian masks is usually restricted to men, but in this tradition they are also worn by girls and young women. Groups of masked dancers gather in the forest, returning to the house of their host to sing, dance and enjoy a big feast. When the ritual is over, the masks become gifts to the initiated girl. All the masks represent strange animals and demons thought up by the person who made them, who is believed to be in communication with spirits or ancestors. Instead of being painted, the eyes are sometimes made of metal sheets, and the masks are fitted with false teeth made of tin.

A stunning gold sun-god mask from the ancient Inca civilization of Peru. ▼

21

Controlling people's actions was another purpose of Amerindian masks, such as those of the Tierra del Fuego Indians who once lived in the southern-most region of Argentina. Men wore masks to represent spirits who were thought to frighten women and make them obedient to men. An ancient legend told of a time when women made the rules and used masks to frighten men. Men were scared of this power so they performed a dance so that women would not gain control again.

Amerindian customs and beliefs have a strong influence on the masking traditions of Hispanic people living throughout the continent. Many of these people are of mixed race, descended from European settlers who took Amerindian wives during the colonial period. Although masks are worn during Christian festivals introduced by Europeans, many of the celebrations still reflect Amerindian beliefs.

Spanish priests, who arrived with the first settlers in the sixteenth century, did not approve of native traditions involving the masks of spirits and ancestors. They forced the Amerindians to adopt Christian festivals and their masks were given horns and renamed 'devils'. In Bolivia, painted devil masks are worn by the tin miners of Oruro, in honour of their favourite Christian saint, the Virgin of Socavon, who is thought to have banished the devil from the community. The fierce-looking masks can be made from carved wood or factory-produced materials like rubber tubing and electric light bulbs.

A Guatemalan dancer dressed ▶ up as a Spanish *conquistador*. Every year thousands of masked dancers act out scenes from the Spanish invasion of the early sixteenth century.

▲ One of Mexico's many festival masks, which are usually worn at religious celebrations. Notice the huge horns decorated with ribbons. With the introduction of Christianity, horns were added to many Amerindian masks to represent devils.

European-style masks are worn in dramatic masquerades such as the masked Dances of the Conquista, which tell of the first meetings between the Spanish *conquistadores* and Amerindian leaders. In Guatemala, these dancers wear realistic wooden face masks of the conqueror Pedro de Alvarado and the native leader, Tecum Uman, as well as of supporting characters such as soldiers and bulls.

In Mexico, most masquerades take place on saints' days or during carnival celebrations. They are also worn by wrestlers with fancy names like Atlantis and Aztec Eagle. Skull and devil masks are worn during the Day of the Dead festival when, once a year, dead souls are thought to return to the world. Children play with toy masks of painted papier mâché and there are also masked dances.

The masks of animal spirits are sometimes made more realistic by adding animal hair, bone, skin or leather, and they often represent water-loving animals such as alligators, fish and serpents. These masks are linked to rain ceremonies, which are very important in many areas of Central America. The Nahua people now wear these masks at Christmas processions, when the animal kingdom is said to worship the infant Jesus. At the same time, some of the ancient meaning still remains: the leading mask is a bat, considered by the Nahua to be the lord

Everybody joins in the Mexican Day of ▶ the Dead celebrations around 1 November. In the villages, simple skeleton masks and traditional hats are worn by groups of dancers.

▲ A spectacular mask-float from the Rio de Janeiro Carnival, constructed from metal pipes and cogs.

of all animals, because it lives in caves which are an important source of fresh water.

In countries all over the continent, masks are worn above all for fun and entertainment, and nowhere are they more lively than at Rio de Janeiro's Mardi Gras carnival in Brazil. This celebration is related historically to the European festivals held before Lent. It is the largest of its kind in the world, involving thousands of people in non-stop dancing and music. People wear fantastic masks and costumes, and high above the crowds the streets are decorated with huge clown and devil masks attached to lamp-posts.

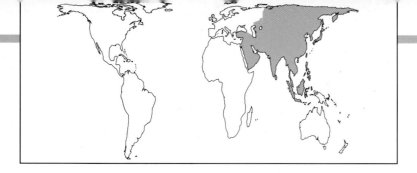

Asia

The variety of masks in Asia reflects the many religions and cultures in its countries. Masks are worn in harvest festival ceremonies in Borneo, 'curing' ceremonies in Sri Lanka, and the Toraja peoples of Sulawesi use funeral masks called *pemia*. Yet Asia is probably best known for its stunning theatrical masks. Japan, India, Thailand, Java and Bali all have their own forms of dance-dramas, and masks are an important part of performers' costumes.

The masks worn in a type of Japanese drama called *Noh* are realistic face masks resembling people, spirits and mythical characters. There are five main types of masks: men, women, madmen, gods and demons. The masks help the actors show their characters' feelings to the audience, from affection and passion to anger and cruelty. The skin tones of the mask, the hairstyle, and the shape of the mouth and teeth differ from character to character. One of the best-known masks is of a young woman, Ko-Omote, who is said to be the ideal of Japanese beauty. It has a pale, whitened face, straight black hair and red lips. Even today, these masks are still made with traditional materials. The carved wood is covered in *gofun* (powdered shell) and is painted with Chinese inks and natural dyes.

The masks worn in ▶ Japanese *Noh* dramas help the audience to understand the personality and feelings of each character.

▲ In the larger cities of India, masked *Ramlila* plays are watched by thousands of people in the streets. Each night a new scene is acted out. The last scene portrays the battle between Rama with his monkey army, and the demons led by Ravana.

The historical epic Hindu stories from India, the *Mahabharata* and the *Ramayana,* have had a great influence on masking traditions in Asia. Scenes from the stories are performed in many different masked dramas throughout the region, and not just in India. In India itself, the stories of the hero Rama and his wife Sita, who is captured by Ravana, are popular. Krishna's battles with demons are also acted out, and the god Vishnu appears as Narasinha, in the form of half-man and half-lion. The masked Ganesha, who has the head of an elephant and a small human body, usually appears at the beginning of each play as he is believed to bring good luck during the performance.

27

Indian theatrical masks are made either from wood that is easy to carve, or modelled in paper and glue, which is placed layer upon layer over a clay mould. Both types of mask are painted with bright colours, including gold and silver, and are then varnished. Mask-makers usually follow set rules when making a mask, and cannot eat certain foods or drink alcohol.

Religious *lama* plays are part of an eight-day festival in Kathmandu, the capital of Nepal. The Nepalese give thanks to the goddess Durga who is believed to help them farm their crops. One of the Durga masks has a crown, and tall poles with flags are attached to the crown in a huge fan shape. The mask can weigh as much as 10 kg. In west Bengal, masks of the goddess Durga are also seen in *Chau* dramas. Here, the fan head-dress is made of materials like tinsel, glass beads, foil and feathers.

▲ A mask-maker from Bali, carving one of the many masks used in the Barong dance dramas.

The stories of the Barong dance dramas from Bali, Indonesia, are also based on the *Ramanyana,* especially the battle between Barong and Rangda. The fantastic wooden masks are brightly painted with bulging eyes. Barong, who is mischievous, usually appears in a dragon, cow or tiger mask. Rangda, who

◄ Rangda is one of Asia's most evil dramatic characters. The tangled hair, fangs and 'fiery' tongue make this a really frightening mask.

▲ These papier mâché masks from Thailand's *Khon* dramas are richly decorated to match the costumes.

is evil, has a mask with fangs, a long, floppy tongue and tangled hair. The tongue, made from a long piece of red cloth, has gold leather flames decorating it. The mask is worn by one man, with the other performers acting as the back legs, rather like a pantomime horse seen in Britain.

Some of the most exotic masks of South-east Asia are found in Thailand's *Khon* dramas. All the roles, except those of the main heroines, are played by men. While the heroines wear just make-up on their faces, the men get the chance to wear spectacular masks. The masks are made from papier mâché, and the tall head-dresses are carved from wood. The demon masks are usually painted gold, with beautiful greens and reds, and have tiny mirrors, coloured glass and mother-of-pearl decorating them.

Sri Lanka is well known for its 'curing' masks. According to tradition, certain evil spirits cause different illnesses. Today, ritual ceremonies called *sanni yakuma* are performed with dancers wearing wooden *sanni* masks. There are about eighteen different types of mask, each for a spirit responsible for an illness, such as fever, shivering or deafness. The mask for vomiting is coloured blue and has a crooked mouth and squashed nose. The ill person is placed at the centre of the masquerade, and the illness is believed to be driven from the body when he or she sees the masked 'spirit'.

In Borneo, harvest festival masks, called *Hudo* masks, are worn during a dance feast of the Dayak peoples who live in the rainforests and on the southern coast. Rice is the main food of the Dayaks, and there are several ceremonies connected with the sowing, growing and harvesting of the crop. *Hudo* masked dances are seen as a way of protecting the newly sown rice from evil spirits. The human, animal, bird, monkey and crocodile masks worn during the dances have large eyes, and some have ears like butterfly wings or large earrings.

In Sri Lanka, the colour of masks is very ▲ important; light colours represent wealthy characters, and reds and greens are for demons.

30

Children are sometimes included in the making and wearing of masks in Asia. Chinese people, particularly from Hong Kong, celebrate their new year with long festivities. Each Chinese year is named after a particular animal, like the rat, the hare, or the pig. Children join in the fun at new year by wearing masks of that year's animal. Children in Madhya Pradesh in India make masks from the skins of large fruit called gourds, which they wear at the popular children's *Cherta* festival. They have large slots for eyes and the teeth are made from grains of rice.

31

Project: Making a Durga Mask

You will need:
Large, stiff cardboard box
Pencil
Scissors
Paints
Paintbrushes
Tin foil
Elastic
5 thin dowel rods, 20 cm long
Masking tape
Glitter
Silver tinsel
Glue
Shells
Recycled items: milk-bottle tops, screwed-up magazine paper, small yoghurt pots

1 Draw on the cardboard an oval shape to fit your face, and above this draw a circle with a curved point at the top. Cut out the whole shape, and cut eyeholes in the face part.

2 Paint and decorate the face of the mask, covering the top part in tin foil. Pierce holes at the sides with scissors and tie the elastic through each hole.

3 Take your wooden dowels and stick them with masking tape, at regular intervals, to the back of the tin foil head-dress part of the mask.

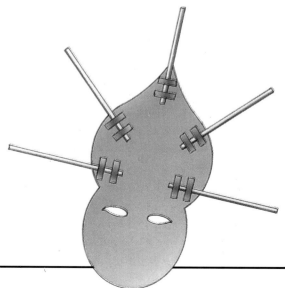

4 Turn the mask to the front again. Tie the tinsel on your first dowel rod, then wind it around the next dowel, and then the next, and so on. Then go back again, until you have gone backwards and forwards three times. Tie the tinsel at the end. Glue all your recycled materials and glitter on to the tinsel and the tin foil part of the head-dress.

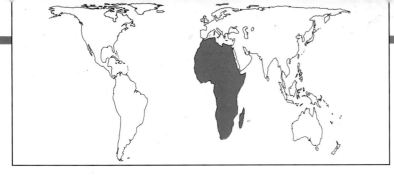

Africa

The African continent covers a vast area and is home to many different peoples, each with its own way of life and language. There are a great variety of African masks. The designs and materials reflect the regions they come from. The use of natural materials – cowrie shells, wood, raffia, animal skins and bark cloth – is part of the African masking tradition, and the wood-carving is extremely skilful. It has been said that the importance of masks to Africa was like the importance of cathedrals to Europe.

These masks are worn ▶ by the Yoruba people of Nigeria during the *gelede* masquerade, in which the powerful life-force of women is celebrated.

Main picture: Masks in Africa often depict animals. This man from the Dogon people of Mali is wearing a mask representing a lizard.

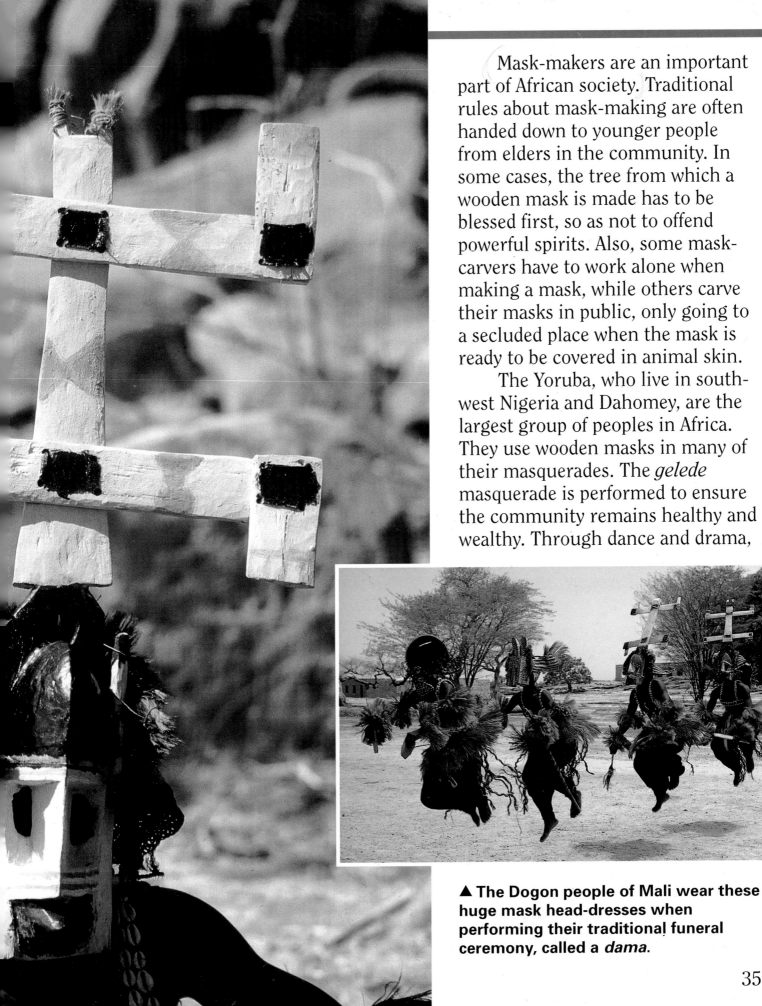

Mask-makers are an important part of African society. Traditional rules about mask-making are often handed down to younger people from elders in the community. In some cases, the tree from which a wooden mask is made has to be blessed first, so as not to offend powerful spirits. Also, some mask-carvers have to work alone when making a mask, while others carve their masks in public, only going to a secluded place when the mask is ready to be covered in animal skin.

The Yoruba, who live in south-west Nigeria and Dahomey, are the largest group of peoples in Africa. They use wooden masks in many of their masquerades. The *gelede* masquerade is performed to ensure the community remains healthy and wealthy. Through dance and drama,

▲ The Dogon people of Mali wear these huge mask head-dresses when performing their traditional funeral ceremony, called a *dama*.

35

masked figures give thanks to the 'mother' spirits, as they are known, which can be either creative and encouraging or angry and destructive. Some *gelede* masks have two parts, a realistic face below and a huge sculpture on top. The mask is hollowed out and rests on top of the dancer's forehead, covering the upper part of the face. The lower half of the face is covered with material. There are many traditional styles and sometimes the sculpture shows groups of figures at work or scenes from history. More recently, rock bands, motor bikes and women using sewing machines have been carved.

East of the Yoruba, the Obuele and Abua Igbo peoples still hold water-spirit ceremonies to appeal for good fortune. A water-spirit mask has a combination of features: partly human and partly crocodile, shark or hippopotamus. It is large and horizontal, and when the wearer walks in water during the ceremony, the mask appears to float on the surface.

Animal and bird masks are worn at the funeral ceremonies of the Dogon peoples of Mali. All Dogon men become members of a masked dancing society called *Ava*. A few years after the death of a respected village member, a funeral ceremony called a *dama* is held.

Funerals are seen by the Dogon as a time to celebrate the joy of living, rather than the sadness of death. During the procession, the performers act out a ritual where they pretend to take the soul of the dead person to the edge of the village and throw it into the bushes. It is believed that the soul will find its way to join other dead family members.

This is a mask from the ▶ Ivory Coast. In Africa, masks often represent animal spirits.

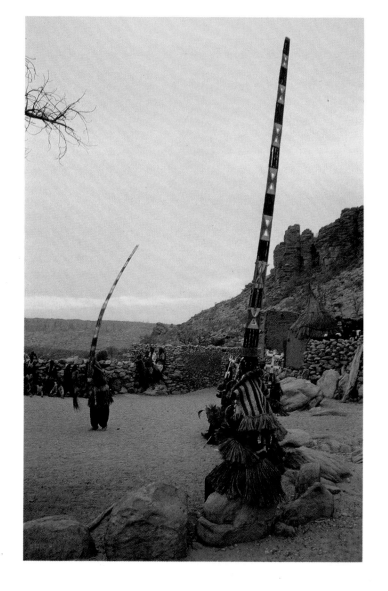

These 'tree' masks from ▶ West Africa are some of the tallest in the world. Imagine trying to balance one on your head while dancing!

sometimes bends to touch the ground with the tip of this blade.

Masked societies like the Dogon's are an important part of the African way of life. The one masking tradition in which only women participate is an initiation ceremony. It is found in Sierra Leone, Liberia and the Ivory Coast. Here, women of the Mende peoples belong to a secret society known as the *Sande*, which is equivalent to a men's secret society called *Poro*. The *Sande* is responsible for the initiation of young girls through the different stages or grades into womanhood. Young girls are taken by the society officials to a quiet place away from the community. At various visits, the girls learn about different topics: child care, craft skills, sexual matters and singing and dancing. Graduation ceremonies are held when the initiates return after each visit. The officials wear beautiful *sowei* masks and celebrate through dance and drama.

Sowei masks are called pot or helmet masks, as they fit completely over the wearer's head and rest on the shoulders. They are made from the trunk of a large tree which is rubbed with palm oil until it is dark and shiny. The carving on the masks shows the Mende's idea of true beauty: a small face, high, rounded forehead, elaborate hairstyle and rolls of fat around the neck, which symbolize wealth. A long raffia costume falls from the mask, covering the whole body, and the dancers move gracefully, communicating only through movement.

The performers at a *dama* wear wooden rectangular masks representing reptiles, birds and animals, which have two large, square eyeholes. A special black and white *kanaga* mask is also worn. It has a tall blade coming from its top, which can be over 2 m high. During the funeral procession, the dancer

Masquerades are also used as a way of making sure there is a good harvest. The British religious song *Lord of the Dance* is based on a masquerade performed by the Senufo peoples from the Ivory Coast. The dance praises their gods for the successful sowing of seeds and asks for the rains to come. All of the Senufo spirits are carved in the wooden masks. Each mask is sacred and is worn by a specially chosen person from the village.

Masks with delicate, detailed . patterns and ornaments using natural materials are still found all over Africa. The Bambara's *n'tomo* mask, modelled on a human face, is worn during ceremonies to prevent illness. It is covered in hundreds of tiny cowrie shells, beads and dried seeds. However, manufactured materials are also having an influence on mask-making. Traditionally, the Chokwe peoples of Zaire and Angola made their fearsome caricature masks from bark cloth, the distorted features being painted on in white clay. Today, such masks are made from old sacking cloth and brown paper.

Masks from the ▶ Chokwe people of Zaire are traditionally made from bark cloth painted with white clay.

◀ Cowrie shells are often
used in African mask-making.

In Africa today, many people ▲
continue the masking tradition by
wearing miniature mask jewellery.

All African masks, however simple, are an
important part of African life and are treated with
respect. In fact, the beautifully polished, black
wooden masks of the Dan Nation of Liberia are
believed to actually *be* the spirits that live in the
mountainside. If a mask is put in the wrong place,
it is believed to frown to show its annoyance.
Masking traditions are very much alive today, and
are being revived more and more as tourists want
to experience the different masquerades of such
varied peoples.

The importance of masks is also shown by the
way many people wear tiny miniature masks as
jewellery or badges. Usually made of precious
metals, clay or wood, they are often given to a bride
by her family on her wedding day as a token of
good luck.

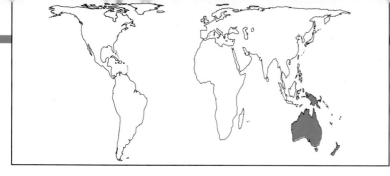

The Pacific

The islands of Melanesia in the South Pacific are the only places in this part of the world which are well known for their masks. These include souvenir masks, dance masks and ancestor spirit masks. There are many remote areas where people still live in a traditional way, following ancient customs involving masks. Although many masks are now produced for tourists by a growing mask-making industry, these modern-day craftspeople still produce masks in traditional styles.

For thousands of years, masking traditions in Melanesia have been an important part of everyday life. Dance masks were once exchanged between different groups during masquerades. Ancestor spirit masks are still worn by some peoples at traditional feasts and rituals. The masks represent these powerful spirits, which have the ability to be helpful or harmful. They assist people to communicate with them, in order to ask for help, or to show respect.

How many different ▶ materials are used to make these Pacific masks?

40

For many years, people have formed special clans, like secret societies, which try to control the power of the spirit world. Members of the clan also make sure that non-members behave properly towards the spirits – especially women and children, who are excluded from the clan. Only men can design, make and wear the masks. Clan members honour their ancestors at special feasts, which are also a time when boys and young men are initiated into the adult life of the clan.

In the Sepik River valley, on the island of Papua New Guinea, masking traditions take place around the men's spirit houses, which are called *tambaran*. There is an enormous variety of masks, with each village having its own style. The most sacred masks are stored in these huge thatched buildings, which have a dance floor nearby. Dancers wear a large, cone-shaped body shroud called a *tumbuan*, representing spirits from the creation of the world. This covers the face and body and has two holes at the side for the arms. Masks of wood or clay depicting mythical ancestors, called *mwai*, are attached to the cone. Some are carved with the tongue sticking out or with gnashing teeth, designed to drive off evil spirits. *Tumbuans* are also used to warn women and children away from an important ceremonial site, or to stop them from eating coconuts being grown for a feast.

In the Maprik and Wosera areas of Papua New Guinea, enormous yams, some up to 200 kg in weight, are kept in the spirit houses, grown especially for ceremonial feasts called *sing sing*. After a successful harvest they are decorated with masks in honour of the spirits of the yam harvest. The masks are made from woven rattan painted in bands of bright colour: red, yellow, black, white and green. The larger masks are worn by dancers, and the smaller masks (less than 30 cm high) are used to decorate the yams.

Gable masks are carved in the river areas of the Middle Sepik, Middle Ramu and the Blackwater Lakes. Large masks made from a variety of leaves, wood and woven cane represent female clan spirits. They are placed on house gables to protect people from disaster, especially illness. It is believed that gable masks are based on a much earlier custom of remodelling human skulls, obtained by headhunting.

In the Papuan Gulf of New Guinea, an *avoko* mask is used to celebrate marriage. This small, round mask has realistic eyes and teeth, and is decorated with seeds and shells. After a husband has brought his wife home for the first time, a clan elder wears the mask in a dance, performed in front of the house, to bring the couple good luck and many children.

Pacific masks are made with all kinds ▶ of animal and plant materials. This miniature mask is made from a turtle shell with cassowary feathers, cowrie shells and fibres from the raffia palm tree.

42

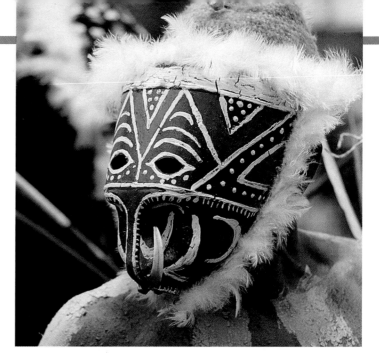

▲ A masked dancer at a ceremonial *sing sing* feast in Papua New Guinea. The mask is surrounded with fine feathers and is painted in sharp bands of colour.

In Papua New Guinea souvenir masks are very common. They are miniature-sized faces, often made from clay or turtle shell, decorated with tiny shells and small tufts of bark. They were once carved into everyday objects, such as canoe paddles, adze handles, house timbers and drums. Today they are often given as gifts or sold to tourists.

Tortoiseshell masks from the small islands of the Torres Straits have a complicated design. They are made from pieces of tortoiseshell, sliced and cut into shapes which are then sewn together with plaited coconut fibre. These are long masks, often made to look like a strange crocodile-fish creature. They were once worn at the annual *horiomu* initiation rituals, when boys and young men learned about the clan, and dancers performed pantomime in front of a screen hung with shells, skulls and statues.

The Fire Dancing Mask is worn by the Baining people from the east of the island of New Britain. This fantastic mask is made of bark cloth sewn on to a rattan frame, with large ears, brightly painted eyes of red and black, and an open mouth. It is worn tilted back at an angle so the dancer can see through the mouth, and is intended to drive away evil spirits thought to be dangerous to growing children.

In the north of the island of New Ireland, the *Malanggan* ceremonies use masks called *tatanua*. People commemorate the death of a chief, some time after he has died, with a second burial ceremony. This marks the building of a new *Malanggan* house, and is also a time for initiation. These ceremonies are very competitive, as each clan tries to get hold of more pigs and yams than there were at the last feast. During this period the young men and boys stay away from the village, but at the final feast they return wearing the *tatanua* mask.

Tatanua masks are very fierce-looking, with lifelike eyes made from snail shells. They have carved wooden faces stained red, black and white, and a high, curved head-dress, made from plant fibres, bark cloth or modern cloth, stiffened with white chalk. Sticks, seeds or other twisted fibres are secured into a series of panels reaching up to a high crest, like the helmet of a Roman centurion or the head of a fabulous bird.

A fearsome *tatanua* mask. Notice how ▶ lifelike the eyes look.

44

Melanesian masks were traditionally made using stone axes and adzes, with skins of lizards and sharks or coral and shell being used to smooth the surfaces. Some were then coated with a mixture of clay, burnt lime and tree oil, while others were polished with a pig's tusk or just painted. Traditionally, natural pigments were used: lime for white, charcoal for black, soapstone for grey, ochres for yellow and brown, and plants for red and blue. Today masks are decorated with modern dyes and paints.

Masks can completely disguise the identity of their wearer. But if we look closely at traditional masks, they can reveal all sorts of things about who the wearer is and where he or she comes from. Next time you wear a mask to a fancy dress party or for Hallowe'en, remember that you are carrying on a tradition that is about 10,000 years old!

If you are making your own mask, ▶ you could use wool for the hair.

Glossary

Adze - a cutting tool with an arched blade.

Alderbark - bark from an alder tree.

All Hallows' Eve - 31 October, the day before All Saints' Day. It is now called Hallowe'en.

Amazon Basin - a vast area of land stretching out from the Amazon river.

Amerindians - the first people to live in Central and South America, before the arrival of Europeans.

Amphitheatres - Theatres with rows of seats built one above another.

Ancestor - a dead relative from very ancient times.

Archaeologists - scientists who study the remains of ancient civilizations.

Bark cloth - a type of cloth made from the bark of a tree.

Burrs - the prickly parts of certain plants.

Caribou - North American reindeer.

Caricature - an exaggerated likeness, usually of a person.

Celts - people who lived in Britain before the Romans.

Clan - a collection of families, who are set apart from others and have a common ancestor.

Colonial period - a time when people from another country govern a region. In this case the governors are the Spanish and Portuguese settlers.

Conquistadores - Spanish and Portuguese conquerors from the early sixteenth century.

Elders - repected older members of a community.

Epic - a very long poem about heroic deeds.

Fertility - being able to produce fruit or crops in great quantity.

Fibres - fine strands, usually from plants or animals, which can be made into material.

Gable - the triangular part of a wall where it meets the roof.

Gondola - a banana-shaped boat which is the traditional form of transport in Venice.

Gourd - a large hard-skinned fruit.

Hispanic - Spanish, in this case Spanish-speaking peoples.

Initiation - a time when a child is prepared at a special ceremony to begin their adult life.

Lent - the 40 days before the Easter festival, when Christians go without certain foods or other favourite things in memory of Jesus Christ.

Manufactured - something which is made, often used to mean something made in a factory on a large scale.

Masquerade - a performance of dancers disguised by wearing masks.

Medieval - a period of history known as the Middle Ages.

Migrants - people who move themselves and their families to live in a different part of the world.

Migration - the movement of people and their families from one part of the world to another.

Mother-of-pearl - smooth shiny shell, which is part of an oyster.

Mythical - something or someone from ancient traditional stories about gods or heroes.

Ochres - mixtures of clay and iron products, like iron oxide.

Pigments - colours made from natural things like plants and soils.

Professionals - people who are paid for their work.

Rattan - cane made from the thin stems of a palm tree.

Reb seeds - seeds from an exotic African plant.

Renaissance - a period of new art and learning. In history this period came after the Middle Ages.

Represent - when one thing is used as a sign of something else.

Ritual - a series of actions which are always repeated at traditional ceremonies.

Sacred - a person or thing with special

importance - often linked with a religious belief.

Secret Society - a clan-like group of people, with secret rules and knowledge.

Shakespearian - the works of the famous 16th-century English playwright, William Shakespeare.

Shaman - a much-respected person with special powers and knowledge of the spirit world.

Shroud - a long piece of material covering the body.

Spanish Conquests - the 16th-century invasion by Spanish armies of Central and South America.

Stencilled - decorated using cut-out patterns.

Trance - a strange feeling - like being in a dream.

Tricorn - a three-cornered hat.

Varnished - painted with a hard shiny lacquer.

Books to Read

Masks, Lyndie Wright (Franklin Watts, 1989)

Festivals, Jeanne McFarland (Macdonald Educational, 1985)

Peoples of the World, Roma Trundle (Usborne, 1990)

Summer Festivals, Mike Rosen (Wayland, 1990)

Theatrical Costume, Miriam Moss (Wayland, 1988)

Traditional Costume, Miriam Moss (Wayland, 1988)

Index

The masks in this book come from many different peoples, represent many things and are used in all sorts of ways. The 'masks' entry in this index lists the main mask designs. If you want to see how masks are used, look at the 'ceremonies', 'dramas' and 'dances' entries. You can use the 'peoples' entry to look up masks from each of the cultures mentioned in the book. If you are making a mask and you need some ideas for things to use, look at the 'materials' section.